WRITTEN AND ILLUSTRATED BY:
MIKE CANINO

FIRST EDITION
COPYRIGHT 2018
ALL RIGHTS RESERVED

CONTENTS

INTRODUCTION

Nymphing is when a fly pattern is fished below the water's surface. The fly patterns usually imitate aquatic insects in their subsurface, pre-adult life cycle stage. Nymphing often requires the use of split shot weights and strike indicators. Split shot weights aid in sinking a nymph pattern to the river bottom. Strike indicators suspend a nymph pattern at a desired water depth and also indicate when a fish strikes or takes your nymphs. Dry fly fishing differs from nymphing because weight and strike indicators are not used, and dry fly patterns usually imitate aquatic insects in their surface, adult life cycle stages. Nymphing is more effective than dry fly fishing because trout mainly feed beneath the water's surface, with the majority of a trout's diet consisting of aquatic insects in their pre-adult, nymph stage (see: **GENERAL AQUATIC INSECT LIFE CYCLE & KEY SPECIES** pg. 12). For the purpose of this book, the terms fly patterns, flies, nymph patterns, and nymphs are used interchangeably.

Nymphing is a simple and easy fly fishing method that anyone can learn. In this guide book, we will use straightforward explanations and illustrations to break down the processes of nymphing into basic concepts. First, we walk you through the necessary nymphing gear, knots, rigs, and flies. Second, we will explain the biology of trout and the life cycle of the major aquatic insects that trout prey upon. Third, we will show you how to locate trout in any stream type, condition, and season. Lastly, we will teach you how to approach and catch trout in any section of a river - and so much more!

FLY ROD & REEL

5- or 6-weight, nine-foot rods are excellent for nymphing, but almost any weight rod will work sufficiently. A heavier weighted fly rod will make casting heavy nymphing rigs easier, but will make playing a trout less exciting. Pick your rod based on your personal preference and the size of the stream you will fish.

Any fly reel is sufficient for nymphing; just make sure you set your drag appropriately in case a big fish decides to run!

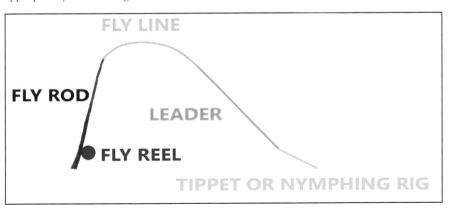

Figure 1: TYPICAL FLY ROD AND REEL SETUP

KNOTS
Necessary nymphing knots, how to tie them, and when to use them.

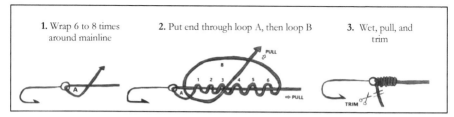

1. Wrap 6 to 8 times around mainline

2. Put end through loop A, then loop B

3. Wet, pull, and trim

Figure 2: IMPROVED CLINCH KNOT: Tying nymphs to leader or tippet.

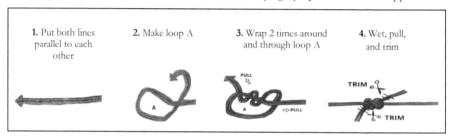

1. Put both lines parallel to each other

2. Make loop A

3. Wrap 2 times around and through loop A

4. Wet, pull, and trim

Figure 3: SURGEON'S KNOT: Tying two pieces of tippet or leader together.

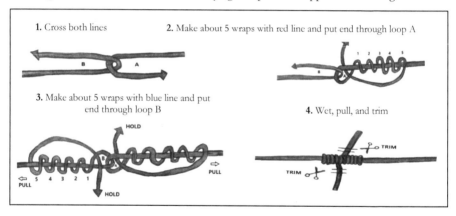

1. Cross both lines

2. Make about 5 wraps with red line and put end through loop A

3. Make about 5 wraps with blue line and put end through loop B

4. Wet, pull, and trim

*Figure 4: BLOOD KNOT: Tying two pieces of tippet or leader together.

*A surgeon's knot is easier and faster to tie than a blood knot and can be substituted if desired

Use your mouth to wet knots when tying and always pull each knot to test its strength, especially with fluorocarbon line because it easily slips.

Trim knots to leave about a half centimeter tag end. A knot with a long tag end will cause your nymphs to drift and look unnatural, while too short of a tag end may slip free during a strike or snag.

LEADER & TIPPET

Leader: The main, clear fishing line that connects the fly line to the fly. 4X or 5X, tapered leaders are excellent for nymphing every trout stream and condition. Short, nine foot leaders are also very easy to cast (see: **Figure 5**).

Tippet: Additional clear fishing line that can be added to the end of a leader or used to tie the components in a nymphing rig. Carrying tippet in sizes from 4X to 6X will prepare you for almost every situation (see: **Figure 6**).

Figure 5:
FLUOROCARBON
TAPERED LEADERS

LEADER & TIPPET

SIZE	DIAMETER (INCHES)	POUND TEST
7X	0.004	2.5
6X	0.005	3.5
5X	0.006	5
4X	0.007	6
3X	0.008	8

Figure 7: LEADER & TIPPET SIZE

Figure 6:
FLUOROCARBON TIPPET

🐟 Use fluorocarbon leader and tippet fishing line over regular nylon monofilament fishing line; fluorocarbon line is less visible to a fish and more resistant to abrasions.

🐟 You can use a heavier pound test leader or tippet (3X or 4X) in water that is high, fast, and murky, or in streams with minimal angling pressure because fish have less time to analyze your fly, decreased visibility, and are less accustomed to seeing fishing line and artificial flies.

🐟 Use a lighter pound test leader or tippet (5X or 6X) in water that is low, slow, and clear, or in streams with substantial angling pressure because fish have more time to analyze your fly, increased visibility, and are more accustomed to seeing fishing line and artificial flies.

🐟 Avoid 7X tippet because it is only slightly less visible to a fish than 6X tippet, and commonly breaks when casted, snagged, or playing a fish.

🐟 The lowest part of your nymphing rig is the most likely part of your rig to snag the bottom. Tie tippet in the order of decreasing pound test from top to bottom to ensure that you will not lose the entire rig if the lowest part of the rig breaks during a snag (see: **NYMPHING RIGS** pg. 6).

WEIGHT

Carrying a split shot pack containing several different weight sizes will prepare you for any type of water current (see: **Figure 8**).

The split shot weights on your nymphing rig should gently bounce or tap along the river bottom every couple of seconds while drifting downstream. If your split shots never tap the bottom, you are *not using enough weight*. If your split shots are frequently standing still on the bottom, *you are using too much weight*.

Figure 8:
SPLIT SHOT PACK

Add and remove split shot to your nymphing rig as needed. A run on a particular river may require five split shots, while a pool only ten yards downstream may require only one split shot.

Several small split shots are less likely to snag the bottom and are easier to wiggle free when snagged compared to one, very large split shot (see: **Figure 9**).

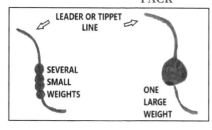

Figure 9: SMALL SPLIT SHOT COMPARED TO LARGE SPLIT SHOT

Try to use round split shots over split shots with easy-to-open tabs. Easy-to-open tab split shots tend to drift less naturally, twist your rig and line, and snag the bottom more than round split shots (see: **Figures 10A & 10B**).

Figure 10A:
ROUND SPLIT SHOT

Figure 10B:
EASY-TO-OPEN TAB SPLIT SHOT

You can apply liquid sinket to your nymphs and line below the strike indicator to help keep your nymphs submerged underwater (see: **Figures 11 & 12**). This is not a crucial step, but is helpful when nymphing without any weight -such as when using the dry fly attractor nymph rig (see: **Dry Fly Attractor Nymph Rig** pg. 9).

Figure 11:
LIQUID SINKET

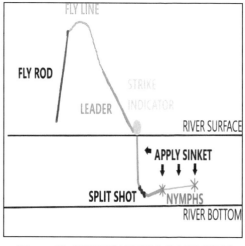

Figure 12: APPLICATION OF SINKET

[4]

STRIKE INDICATORS (SI)

| THINGAM-ABOBBER | YARN | TWISTABLE FOAM | AIR-LOCK | FOAM STICK-ON | CORK | JAM STOP THINGAM-ABOBBER |

Figure 13: SEVERAL TYPES OF STRIKE INDICATORS

Strike indicators (SI) come in many different shapes and sizes (see: **Figure 13**) and suspend your nymphs at a specific depth underwater and help you detect when a fish strikes. If you don't use a SI, many strikes will go undetected because it will be difficult for you to see when a fish takes your nymphs.

Buoyancy and *adjustability* are the most important factors to consider when selecting a SI. Buoyancy is important because you do not want the SI to sink below the water's surface. Adjustability is important because you frequently need to adjust your SI up and down the length of your leader.

No SI is perfect for every situation, but we highly recommend using and carrying the yarn indicator or air-lock indicator in several sizes (see: **Figure 13**). Yarn indicators are buoyant, highly sensitive, and unlikely to scare fish because they land softly on the water's surface; however, they can create twists in your leader when adjusted. Air-lock indicators are extremely buoyant and adjustable, but are less sensitive and can scare fish because they tend to splash down hard on the water's surface.

To decrease the chance of spooking fish by disturbing the water's surface with your SI, use the smallest SI that still maintains buoyancy.

You frequently need to adjust your SI according to the water depth you are fishing. Depending on which nymphing rig type you are using, attach the SI to your leader one and a half to three times the depth of water, i.e., if fishing in two feet of water, the SI should be three to six feet from the bottom of your nymphing rig (see: **NYMPHING RIGS** pg. 6). You may need to adjust your SI several times in just one particular section of a river.

You can apply liquid floatant to the beginning of your leader all the way to the SI to help keep the SI and leader afloat. This is not a crucial step, but is helpful when using a yarn SI (see: **Figures 14 & 15**).

Figure 14: LIQUID FLOATANT

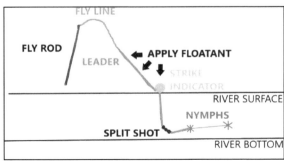

FLY LINE

FLY ROD

LEADER

APPLY FLOATANT

STRIKE INDICATOR

RIVER SURFACE

NYMPHS

SPLIT SHOT

RIVER BOTTOM

Figure 15: APPLICATION OF FLOATANT

NYMPHING RIGS

Three most common nymphing rigs, advantages and disadvantages of each, how to tie them, when to use them, and other tips.

STANDARD NYMPH RIG

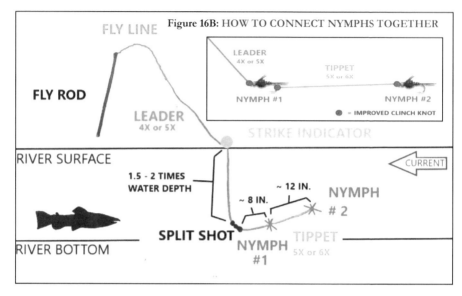

Figure 16A: HOW TO TIE A STANDARD NYMPH RIG

ADVANTAGES: Easy to tie, cast long distances, and switch to a dry fly rig.

DISADVANTAGES: Easily snags the bottom, drifts less naturally, and does not sink to the bottom as quickly as a bounce nymph rig (see: **Bounce Nymph Rig** pg. 7). You do not know the exact level in the water column your nymphs are drifting at.

BEST FOR: Beginners, shallow riffles and runs, shallow to moderately deep pools, pocket water, tailouts of pools, and flats (see: **TROUT LOCATIONS** pg. 16).

Bead head nymphs help sink your nymphs down to the river bottom and work better with this rig than non-bead head nymphs.

Use two nymphs at once if you are capable and regulations permit. Using two nymphs at once will help you to quickly pinpoint the fish's feeding preferences; however, two nymphs have a tendency to tangle more than one nymph.

The tippet section between nymph # 2 and nymph # 1 should be tied with a lighter pound test line than the leader. Tying the rig in this manner ensures that if nymph # 2 snags the bottom, it will break off before nymph # 1, and you will only lose one nymph instead of two nymphs (see: **Figure 16B**).

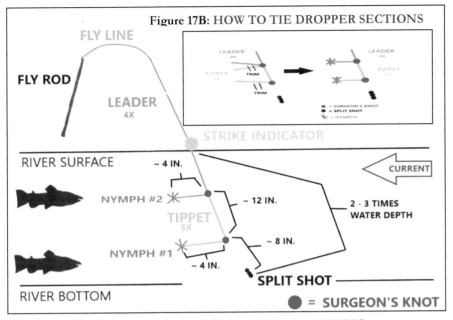

Figure 17B: HOW TO TIE DROPPER SECTIONS

Figure 17A: HOW TO TIE A BOUNCE NYMPH RIG

ADVANTAGES: Drifts more naturally, sinks to the bottom quicker, and less likely to snag the bottom compared to a standard nymph rig. Effectively fishes for entirety of a drift because the nymphs sink quickly and are at the exact desired level from the bottom. Nymphs do not get covered as much in algae-rich streams.

DISADVANTAGES: Time consuming to tie and retie if part of the rig breaks. Difficult to cast long distances.

BEST FOR: All water types except for slow, shallow pools, and pocket water. Excellent in a fast river run.

Although you can use bead head nymphs with this rig, non-bead head nymphs work better because they are less likely to tangle.

Use two nymphs at once if you are capable and regulations permit to quickly pinpoint the fish's feeding preferences. Nymph # 1 and # 2 are unlikely to tangle with each other because the dropper lengths are shorter than the space between each nymph (see: **Figure 17A**).

The nymph # 1 and # 2 four inch dropper sections should be tied with a lighter pound test tippet line than the tippet section that contains the split shots. Tying the rig in this manner ensures that if the split shot tippet section snags the bottom, it will break off before the nymph dropper sections (see: **Figure 17A**).

BOUNCE NYMPH RIG ADJUSTMENTS

Several adjustments can be made to the bounce nymph rig for easier use if desired. You can make some, or all of the adjustments described below (see: **Figure 18**).

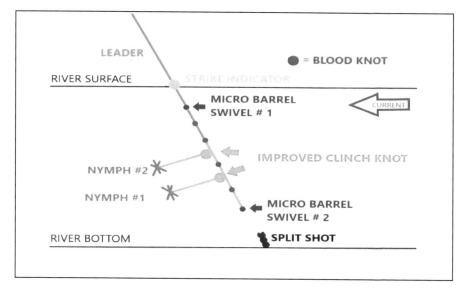

Figure 18: BOUNCE NYMPH RIG ADJUSTMENTS

Micro barrel swivel # 1 prevents the rig from twisting your leader and makes for easy removal of the rig when switching to a dry fly rig.

Micro barrel swivel # 2 prevents the rig from twisting and makes for easy retying of the split shot tippet section if it breaks off. The split shot tippet section is the part of the rig most likely to snag in rocks or other debris because it drags on the bottom.

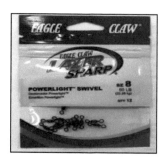

Figure 19: MICRO BARREL SWIVELS

Several blood knot sections can be tied at all different levels below the strike indicator as needed. For example, if trout are feeding near the surface during a dry fly hatch, you could attach a nymph to a blood knot section about twelve inches below your strike indicator to imitate an emerging aquatic insect (see: **General Aquatic Insect Life Cycle & Key Species** pg. 12).

The knots of each blood knot section prevent the nymph droppers from sliding up and down the rig. If you do not tie blood knots, the nymph droppers would slide up and down the rig when casted or playing a fish.

DRY FLY ATTRACTOR NYMPH RIG
(also known as "dry-dropper" or "hopper-dropper" rig)

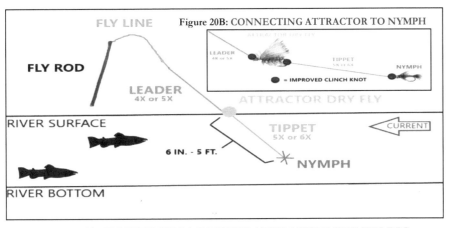

Figure 20A: HOW TO TIE A DRY FLY ATTRACTOR NYMPH RIG

ADVANTAGES: Simultaneously fish two different insect species, life stages, and levels in the water column at once. Easy to cast long distances.

DISADVANTAGES: The nymph often does not sink deep enough into the bottom strike zone. The attractor fly is often difficult to keep afloat. You do not know the exact level in the water column your nymph is drifting in.

BEST FOR: Middle to late summer when large terrestrial insects are present, during a dry fly hatch, shallow water, and pocket water.

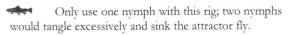 Use a buoyant attractor fly to ensure it stays afloat. Use a bead head nymph to ensure the nymph sinks below the water's surface. Popular dry flies to use with this rig include an elk hair caddis and grasshopper (see: **Figures 21 & 22**).

Figure 21: GRASSHOPPER DRY FLY

Only use one nymph with this rig; two nymphs would tangle excessively and sink the attractor fly.

During a caddisfly hatch, use an emerging nymph such as a soft hackle hare's ear nymph (see: **FLIES** pg. 10) beneath a caddis dry fly.

Do not add split shot to the tippet section below the attractor fly because it will sink the dry fly.

Figure 22: ELK HAIR CADDIS DRY FLY

Apply floatant to the leader and attractor fly. Apply sinket to the nymphs and tippet beneath the attractor fly (see: **Figures 12 & 15** pgs. 4 & 5).

FLIES
The only five nymph patterns you need.

1. Gold-Ribbed Hare's Ear Nymph

SIZES: # 12, 14, 16, 18
IMITATES: mayfly nymphs, caddis larvae, caddis pupae, scuds, sow bugs, large stonefly nymphs

2. Pheasant Tail Nymph

SIZES: # 12, 14, 16, 18
IMITATES: mayfly nymphs, midge larvae, midge pupae, small stonefly nymphs

3. Prince Nymph

SIZES: # 12, 14, 16
IMITATES: mayfly nymphs, caddis larvae, stonefly nymphs, sow bugs, emerging nymphs

4. Copper John Nymph

SIZES: # 12, 14, 16, 18
IMITATES: mayfly nymphs, stonefly nymphs

5. Zebra Midge Nymph

SIZES: # 16, 18, 20, 22
IMITATES: midge larvae

➤ You do not have to "match the hatch" when you use **Flies 1 through 5** because they imitate every major aquatic insect species that trout feed (see: **GENERAL AQUATIC INSCT LIFE CYCLE & KEY SPECIES** pg. 12). Matching the hatch is when you attempt to use a fly pattern that imitates the exact insect species currently hatching in the river.

➤ Size is the most important factor to consider when selecting a fly pattern. Nymph profile and shape are the second most important factors to consider, while color is last.

➤ Continually rotate nymph patterns and sizes throughout the day until you pinpoint the exact nymph pattern and size the fish prefer. You should change flies at least every hour that you do not get a strike.

Other notable but optional nymph patterns:

6. Soft Hackle Hare's Ear Nymph

SIZES: # 14, 16, 18
IMITATES: emerging mayfly nymphs, emerging caddis nymphs

🐟 Use during a dry fly hatch because it imitates an emerging aquatic insect (see: **GENERAL AQUATIC INSECT LIFE CYCLE & KEY SPECIES** pg. 12).

7. Egg Fly

SIZES: # 12, 14
COLORS: orange, chartreuse, white
IMITATES: trout and suckerfish eggs

🐟 Use during the fall, winter, and spring when fish are spawning and feeding on eggs.

Additional nymph patterns important to Western United States Region:

8. Pat's Rubber Legs
   Nymph

9. LaFontaine Deep
   Sparkle Pupa Nymph

10. San Juan Worm

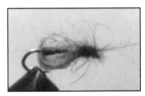

SIZES: # 4, 8, 10, 12
IMITATES: large
stonefly nymphs

SIZES: # 12, 14, 16, 18
IMITATES: caddis
pupae

SIZES: # 8, 10, 12, 14
IMITATES: aquatic
worms

🐟 Flies **8, 9, and 10** imitate insects which are more common to the Western United States and should be used in addition to **flies 1 through 7** in that region.

🐟 Flies **1 through 10** can be used in both bead head and non-bead head forms. Bead head nymphs sink faster than non-bead head nymphs, and tend to work best with a standard nymph rig and dry fly attractor nymph rig. Non-bead head nymphs work best with the bounce nymph rig (see: **NYMPHING RIGS** pgs. 6-9).

GENERAL AQUATIC INSECT LIFE CYCLE & KEY SPECIES

The major aquatic insects that trout prey upon are classified into four main categories: mayflies, caddisflies, stoneflies, and midges. Each category contains many species, but all species within a category have a similar life cycle (see: **Figures 23 A, B, & C**).

The majority of an aquatic insect's life is spent in the subsurface, nymph life cycle stage. Nymphing is almost always more effective than dry fly fishing because subsurface stages are always available to trout for food while adult, surface stages are not.

While adults of each insect category look very different from each other, each category have similar looking nymph stages. Many of the recommend flies from the previous section imitate nymph species in multiple categories at once.

"Matching the hatch" is unnecessary if you use the nymphs from the previous section because the patterns imitate the four main categories of aquatic insects in their subsurface life stages (see: **FLIES** pg. 10). All you have to do is rotate between the nymph patterns from the previous section until you figure out which pattern the fish are feeding on.

Nymphing when trout are rising and feeding on adult, surface insects is still an effective tactic because trout also feed on emerging insects during a hatch. In many cases, trout feed more heavily on emerging insects than their adult counterparts, and many of the nymph patterns from the previous section also imitate emerging nymphs.

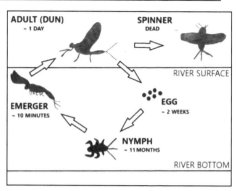

Figure 23A: MAYFLY LIFE CYCLE & TIME IN EACH STAGE

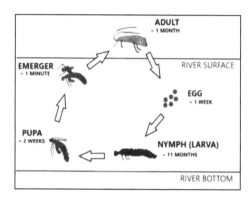

Figure 23B: CADDISFLY AND MIDGE LIFE CYCLE & TIME IN EACH STAGE*

*Only caddisfly illustrated in diagram

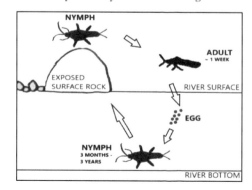

Figure 23C: STONEFLY LIFE CYCLE & TIME IN EACH STAGE

[12]

TROUT VISION - AND WHY IT'S IMPORTANT

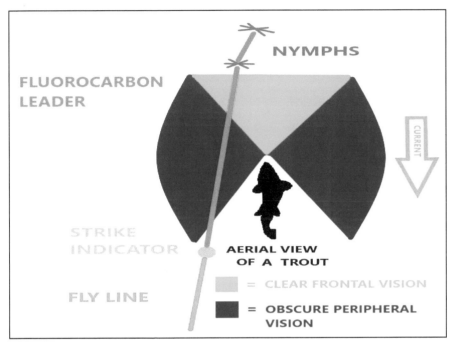

Figure 24: A TROUT'S FIELD OF VISION

 Trout *clearly see objects that are directly in front of them* (see: **Figure 24;** green shading). The distance they can see in front of them depends on water clarity, and is usually limited to within three feet. In order for a trout to see your fly patterns, they need to drift directly in front of a fish.

 Trout *cannot clearly see objects that are located to their side* (see: **Figure 24;** gray shading). Trout will not move sideways much to take your fly patterns because they cannot clearly see them.

 Approach from downriver as much as possible to avoid spooking fish because trout have a blind spot directly behind them.

 Since fluorocarbon leader and tippet are basically invisible to a fish, but strike indicators and fly line are visible, you only want your leader and nymphs within a trout's field of vision. Ideally, the strike indicator and fly line should land and drift outside of a trout's field of vision to avoid spooking it (see: **Figure 24**).

 Make sure your flies do not drift underneath a trout because trout look up and cannot see anything that is below them.

[13]

Fast water currents, such as those in riffles, runs, and pocket water, disturb the water surface and make it harder for trout to see and hear. This is advantageous to the angler because you are less likely to spook fish while approaching. Additionally, the current can mask many mistakes made in your nymph presentation.

Trout are sensitive to shadows because they have predators of the sky; keep your shadow off the river because it will spook fish.

Murky water decreases the distance a trout can see. However, trout can still see your nymphs well enough to bite, but it may be limited to within a few inches. Under murky conditions, fish bigger, flashier nymphs in black to contrast with the brown water so trout can see your flies easier.

Figure 25: LIGHT REFRACTION AND WHAT TROUT SEE

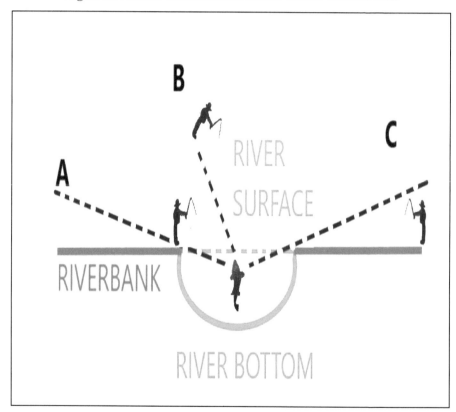

FIGURE EXPLANTATION: Refraction of light in water causes objects to appear closer and more overhead to a fish. Standing within a trout's field of vision, such as standing too close to a fish on the riverbank in **position A,** will cause you to actually appear closer and more overhead to a fish (**position B**). Maintain a low profile and stay as far back from a fish as possible, like in **position C,** to stay out of a trout's field of vision.

WATER DYNAMICS

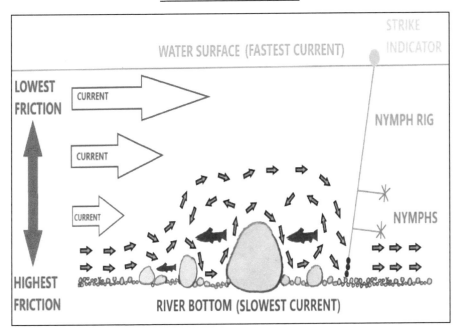

Figure 26: RIVER FRICTION AND WATER CURRENTS

~~~< Due to friction with the river bottom, water currents decrease in speed from the surface to the bottom of a river (see: **Figure 26**). The change in current speed can be extreme, and trout can hold on the bottom in areas with incredibly fast surface water.

~~~< More metabolic energy is required for a trout to maintain their position in fast water than in slow water. Trout may temporarily move closer to the surface during a dry fly hatch to more easily feed on surface insects, but the majority of the time, they are *located within one foot of the bottom* where they expend little energy to maintain their position. In many sections of a river, trout only feed on subsurface insects because too much energy is required to rise to surface insects.

~~~< You should always target the bottom water column with your nymphs because that is where almost all fish are located. Your strike indicator should move slightly slower than the surface current because your weight and nymphs are down in the slower, bottom current. If your strike indicator is moving as fast as the surface current, then your nymphs are not near the bottom because you are not using enough weight.

~~~< Large rocks and other structures on the bottom slow down the water and create pockets of slower current. Trout reside in these locations because they expend minimal energy and can quickly ambush prey brought to them by the nearby faster currents (see: **Figure 26**).

TROUT LOCATIONS

The water types listed below are pictured in **Figure 28** *on the following page:*

A. **Pocket Water:** Excellent holding and nymphing area in spring through fall as long as water depths behind rocks are deep enough.

B. **Riffles:** Generally poor holding water unless significantly deep. However, can be excellent nymphing areas during an aquatic insect hatch when fish move into these shallow locations to easily feed.

C. **Runs:** Excellent year-round nymphing water provided there are large enough bottom rocks to shelter fish from fast currents. Trout will also move up from pools into these locations during an aquatic insect hatch to easily feed.

D. **Pools:** Excellent year-round holding water but are often difficult to fish because pools can be very deep and slow, giving fish more time to inspect and reject your nymphs. The majority of trout are located at the head of a pool. Trout will also move down to a pool's tailout during an aquatic insect hatch to easily feed.

E. **Flats:** Poor holding water and often difficult to fish because trout are highly spread out. A very quiet approach is needed to avoid spooking fish because the water is slow and shallow.

F. **Undercut Banks:** Fish are very protected in these locations and can easily move into nearby currents to ambush prey.

G. **Log Jams:** Fish are very protected in these locations. Cast directly below the log jam to minimize snags.

H. **Islands:** The upstream and downstream points of an island often create breaks in the current where fish can hold. Additionally, the downstream point of an island often has a deep hole.

I. **Waterfalls & Dams:** Can be excellent holding water if the water is deep enough. Fish directly below the waterfall or dam in the white water, and downstream until it becomes too shallow to hold fish.

J. **Springs:** Provide stable water temperatures where trout can congregate when water temperatures become too hot in the summer, or too cold in the winter. Look for bubbles consistently floating to the surface in a pool to locate springs.

K. **Tributary Inlets:** Often create a deep drop-off where they first enter a river and can supply fresh, cold water in the hot summer months which attracts fish.

L. **Eddies:** Excellent holding locations. Fish will normally face in the downstream direction of the main river flow because the current is reversed.

M. **Weed Beds:** Fish are very protected in these locations and are also areas with an ample food supply. Fish along the edges of weed bed's to avoid snags.

Figure 28: RIVER AND TROUT HOLDING LOCATIONS

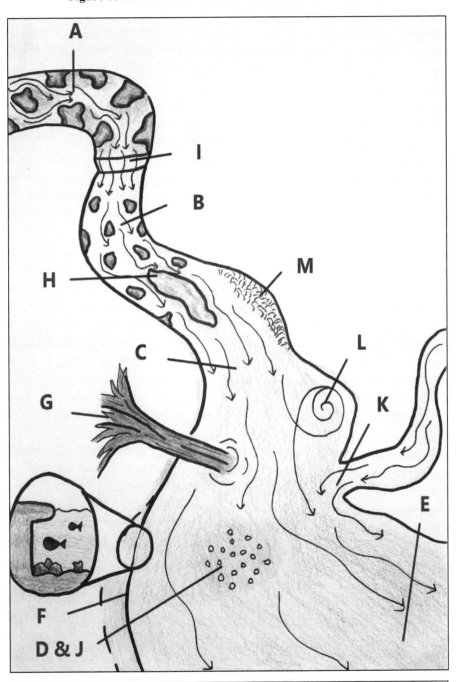

PHOTO ILLUSTRATED BY SARAH DURAN

BUBBLE LINES & CURRENT SEAMS

Bubble lines and current seams typically form wherever currents hit an underwater structure, fast currents meet slow currents, or where deep water meets shallow water. These areas are often excellent holding locations for trout because they provide a break in the current where fish can conserve energy, and currents bring food right to them. These locations can occur anywhere in a river and several examples are shown below (see: **Figures 27A, B, & C**).

Figure 27A: Fish will hold along the seam where the slow currents (A) border the fast currents (B).

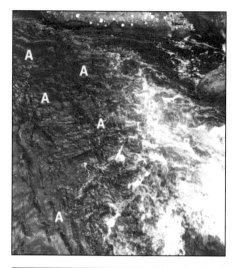

Figure 27B: Fish will hold along the seam where the slow currents (A) border the fast currents (B).

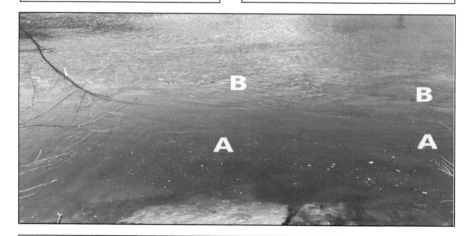

Figure 27C: Fish will hold in the slower, bubble line (A) which borders the faster current seam (B).

TECHNIQUES & APPROACHES
Four systematic approach methods to effectively nymph any stream type.

HIGH STICK WADING METHOD: Preferred method in pocket water, riffles, and shallow runs where you can wade and get close to fish without spooking them.

Figure 29: HIGH STICK WADING METHOD

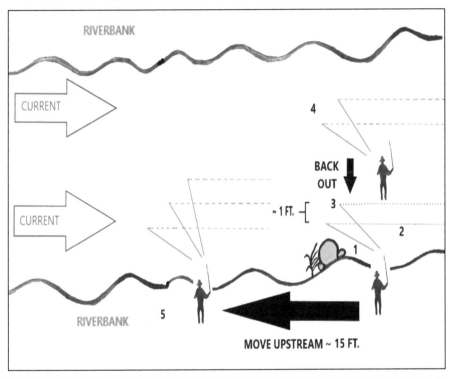

STEP 1: Let out about twenty feet of fly line and cast about forty-five degrees upstream from your position.

STEP 2: Hold your rod tip up high and let your line drift in front of you, then downstream below you. Keep all slack fly line off the water.

STEP 3: Repeat **STEPS 1 & 2** but cast about a foot outwards into the river each time. Do this until you can't cast any further without letting more fly line out from your spool.

STEP 4: Quietly wade a few feet further into the river and repeat **STEPS 1-3** until you reach the other side of the bank, or reach non-wadeable water.

STEP 5: Back all the way out of the river to your original position and move about fifteen feet upstream. Repeat **STEPS 1-5**.

The high stick wading method ensures that you're covering an entire section of a river systematically and evenly because trout can hold anywhere.

It's crucial to keep all slack in your fly line off the water. Ideally, your strike indicator and nymphs below should be the only things touching the water (see: **Figure 30**).

It looks unnatural when the current pulls your strike indicator sideways across the water's surface. You want your strike indicator to drift downstream in a straight line from where it originally landed upstream.

Your strike indicator should drift slightly slower than the surface current which ensures that your nymphs are down on the bottom in the slower current. Add more weight and adjust your strike indicator if necessary (see: **WEIGHT** pg. 4, **WATER DYNAMICS** pg. 15)

Move quietly and deliberately to avoid spooking fish.

Pointing your rod tip high in the air will help you guide your strike indicator downstream, and keep your fly line off the water (see: **Figure 30**).

Figure 30: PHOTO OF HIGH STICK WADING METHOD

CAST & MEND METHOD: Preferred method in deep pools and runs where the water is too deep to wade, or you are unable to get close to the fish without spooking them. Unlike the high stick wading method, you need to let fly line out of your spool each cast to target water that is further away. Your fly line will also float on the water's surface, and you must mend your fly line to keep your nymphs drifting downstream naturally.

Figure 31: CAST AND MEND METHOD

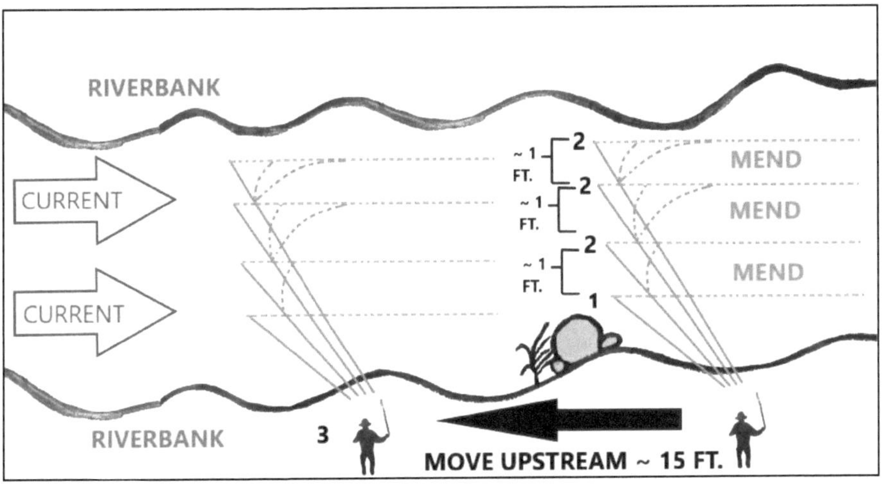

STEP 1: Let out about twenty feet of fly line from your spool and cast about forty-five degrees upstream from your position. Let your line drift in front of you, then downstream below you.

STEP 2: Let about a foot more of fly line from your spool and cast about one foot outwards from your last position. Repeat this process until you can't cast any further, or your presentation drifts unnaturally. You must mend your fly line in order for your presentation to drift naturally (see: **Figures 32 & 33** pg. 23).

STEP 3: Move upstream about fifteen feet and repeat **STEPS 1 & 2**.

It looks unnatural when the current pulls your strike indicator sideways across the water's surface. You want your strike indicator to drift downstream in a straight line from where it originally landed upstream. You must mend your fly line upstream or downstream to accomplish this.

Your strike indicator should drift slightly slower than the surface current which ensures that your nymphs are down on the bottom in the slower current. Add more weight and adjust your strike indicator if necessary (see: **WEIGHT** pg. 4, **WATER DYNAMICS** pg. 15)

Move quietly and deliberately to avoid spooking fish.

UPSTREAM MEND: Perform if faster water is between you and the target area.

Figure 32: UPSTREAM MEND

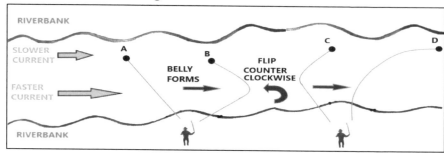

FIGURE EXPLANATION: The faster current will *pull your fly line downstream* faster than your strike indicator which will form a belly in your fly line **(B)**. You must *mend your fly line upstream* by flipping your rod tip counterclockwise **(C)** so your strike indicator floats downstream drag free **(D)**.

DOWNSTREAM MEND: Perform if slower water is between you and the target area.

Figure 32: DOWNSTREAM MEND

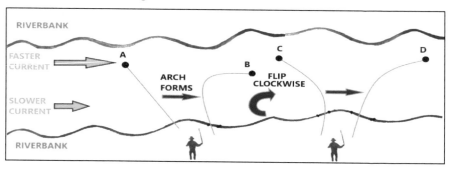

FIGURE EXPLANATION: The faster current will *pull your strike indicator downstream* faster than your fly line which will form an arch in your fly line **(B)**. You must *mend your fly line downstream* by flipping your rod tip clockwise **(C)** so your strike indicator floats downstream drag free **(D)**.

You may need to mend your fly line several times throughout a single drift.

Casting a nymphing rig can be more challenging than casting a dry fly rig because it weighs more. Slow down your casts, and do not make as many false casts with a nymphing rig. Also, let your rig drift completely downstream from you before you cast; the current will apply pressure to your fly line and will lift your rig off the bottom to the surface.

POCKET WATER METHOD: Pocket water often requires a unique approach because the water currents are inconsistent, and short casts are needed to effectively present your nymphs and avoid spooking fish. How you should approach, and the order you should cast to each holding structure in a typical pocket water section is shown below (see: **Figure 34**).

Figure 34: LIKELY ORDER TO TARGET A POCKET WATER SECTION

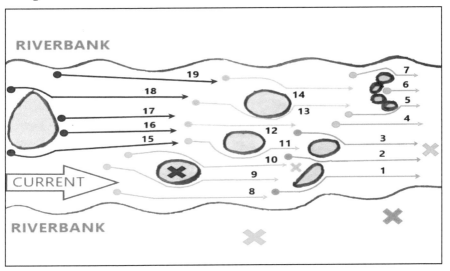

X = position you should stand
CIRCLES = where to cast and land your strike indicator
NUMBERS = order you should cast to avoid spooking fish

◄━━ Underwater structures will disturb the normal current flow and create V or U shapes in the current both above and below a structure where fish will hold (see: **Figures 27A & B** pg. 18).

◄━━ Always cast several feet above each fish holding location to ensure that your nymphs have time to sink to the bottom before they reach a potential fish.

◄━━ Target each holding location deliberately and individually, making short drifts so you don't spook fish in the next location. If your fly line drifts through a location, you likely spooked every fish there. It's best to start close and work your way outward.

◄━━ Try to keep your fly line off the water's surface. Make short drifts and hold your rod tip high in the air so your strike indicator and nymphs are the only things in the water. You want to guide your strike indicator and nymphs around each holding structure.

◄━━ Approach from downstream to stay in the fish's blind spot (see: **Figure 24** pg. 13).

UPSTREAM METHOD: A purely upstream approach may be required in areas where wading or casting from the riverbank is impossible due to overhanging branches or other unavoidable structures. This method may also be required in streams that are too small to cast in front of you without spooking fish, like in small brooks or spring creeks.

You will either have to stand on the riverbank, or wade in the water right next to the riverbank and systematically cast upstream for this method (see: **Figure 35**).

Figure 35: UPSTREAM METHOD

STEP 1: Let about thirty feet of fly line out from your spool and cast directly upstream. Let your nymphs drift back to where you are standing, while simultaneously stripping in the slack fly line as it drifts towards you.

STEP 2: Without letting anymore line out, cast about one foot horizontally from your last cast. Let your nymphs drift back to your standing position. Repeat this process until you reach the opposite side of the river, or non-wadeable water.

STEP 3: Move upstream about ten feet from your position in **STEP 1** and repeat **STEPS 1 & 2.**

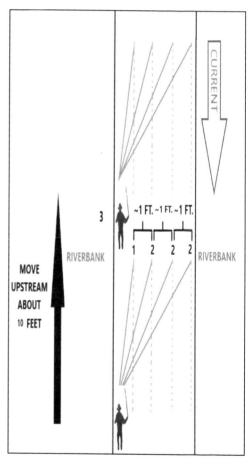

Cast at a slight angle outward so your strike indicator and fly line do not drift directly over any fish and spook them (see: **Figure 24** pg. 13).

Move very quietly to avoid spooking fish because you will cast short distances with this method.

NYMPH MOVEMENT

🐟 The majority of nymph species cannot move or swim throughout the water column and it will look unnatural if you give any movement to your nymphs. However, some nymph species can move and swim throughout the water column and it's appropriate to *very occasionally* give movement to your nymphs by performing the leisenring lift or nymph twitch (see: **Figure 36**).

Figure 36: LEISENRING LIFT AND NYMPH TWITCH LOCATIONS

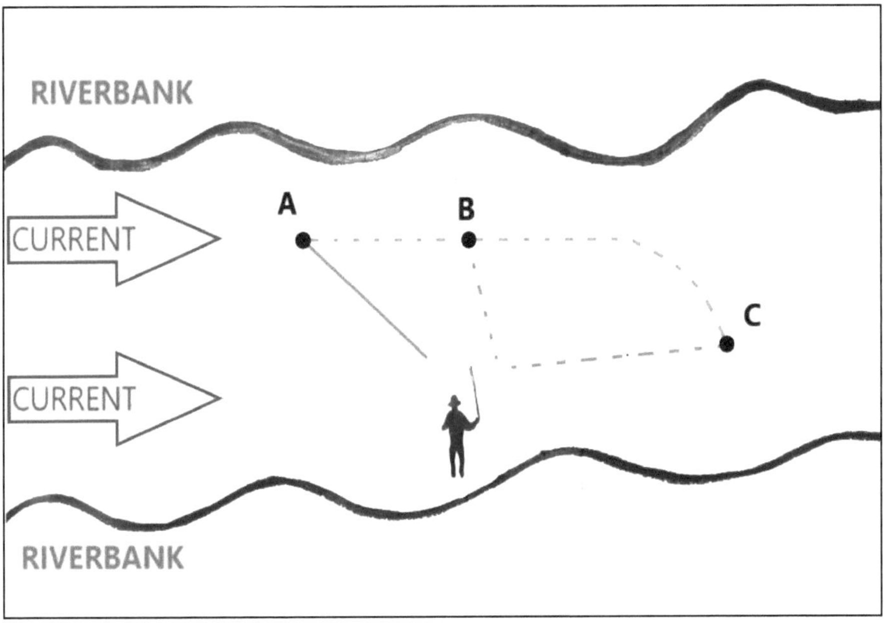

Leisenring Lift: Once your nymphs get to the target area **(B)**, quickly lift your rod tip into the air which will raise the nymphs from the bottom to the surface. Then, quickly lower your rod tip back down so the nymphs sink to the bottom again. This action simulates an emerging nymph rising in the water column to hatch on the river's surface.

Nymph Twitch: Allow your nymphs to hang directly below you at the end of your drift for about five seconds **(C)**, and *slightly* twitch your rod tip a few inches every couple of seconds. This action will give a swimming motion to your nymph patterns, while also simulating an emerging nymph rising in the water column to hatch on the river's surface.

🐟 Perform the leisenring lift and nymph twitch during a caddisfly hatch because many caddis species rapidly rise from the bottom to the water's surface.

MORE APPROACH TIPS

Cover a lot of water. While some water may look good, it may actually be poor fish holding water because of many different reasons: inadequate bottom structures, low oxygen, high water temperatures, and no available food.

Focus on areas that people do not fish heavily, and quickly fish through an area that you know was just fished within the last hour. Trout will stop feeding and retreat for cover when they feel threatened. Trout that are heavily targeted are also smarter and harder to catch.

Remember to change your nymphs often and adjust your weight and strike indicator frequently. This is a constant job (see: **FLIES** pg. 10, **WEIGHT** pg. 4, and **STRIKE INDICATORS** pg. 5)!

Move quietly: even walking on the riverbank can send vibrations throughout the water and spook fish.

Wear natural colors such as brown and green that blend well with the landscape and are less visible to a fish. Do not wear bright neon colored shirts!

Trout in fast water only have a split second to decide if they want to take your nymph, so you can often get away with using bigger and less exact nymph presentations in fast currents. If fish were taking your flies in fast water and are now rejecting them in slower water, try using smaller nymphs or a lighter tippet size.

STRIKE DETECTION

It can be difficult to detect fish strikes when you first begin nymphing because some fish may barely take your fly, causing only a very subtle action to your strike indicator. **Figures 37 A, B, & C** show what will happen to your strike indicator during the most common strike scenarios, and what the fish is doing underwater to cause this action.

Watch your strike indicator as if it were a dry fly. If your strike indicator behaves unnatural in any way, you should set your hook because it could be a fish (see **HOOK SET** pg. 28).

Keep as much slack out of your fly line as possible so you can quickly react if a fish takes your nymphs.

Figure 37A: STIKE INDICATOR PAUSES

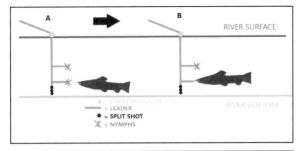

A trout barely moves from its location to take your nymph **(A)**, and remains still while holding your nymph in its mouth **(B)**.

Figure 37B: STRIKE INDICATOR BOPS UNDERWATER

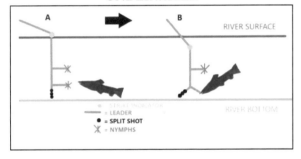

A trout rises off the bottom to take your nymph **(A)**, then retreats straight back downward to the bottom **(B)**.

Figure 37C: STRIKE INDICATOR MOVES SIDEWAYS

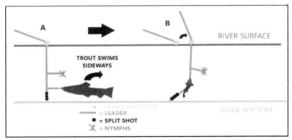

A trout moves sideways from its location to take your nymph **(A)**, then retreats sideways back to its original location **(B)**.

HOOK SET

Only slight pressure is needed to properly set a hook into a trout's mouth. Setting the hook too hard can result in breaking your line, tearing your nymph from the trout's mouth, and spooking fish. How to properly set a hook with a fly rod is shown below (see: **Figure 38**).

Figure 38: HOW TO SET A HOOK

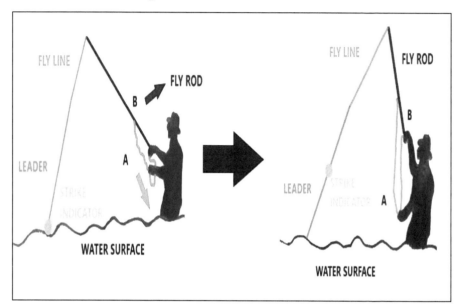

FIGURE EXPLANATION: If you're right handed, use your left hand to strip about one foot of fly line in (A) while simultaneously using your right hand to lift your rod tip up and back (B). This action will take the slack out of your fly line while applying force to the fish.

When fighting a fish, always keep your rod tip pointed in the air approximately forty-five degrees to the fish. However, if a fish jumps, you should lower your rod tip to temporarily give out some slack line so the hook doesn't rip out of the fish's mouth.

If you're consistently missing fish during a strike, you are either not setting the hook fast enough, the strike indicator length is too long, or you have too much slack in your fly line. If you do not set the hook fast enough, it gives a fish enough time to realize your nymph is fake and spit it from its mouth. If your strike indicator length is too long, your strike indicator will be unable to move when the fish takes your nymphs. If you have too much slack in your fly line, you will not be able to apply enough force to set your hook.

DAILY RIVER CHANGES

Trout feeding activity is usually greatest during an aquatic insect hatch. Aquatic insect hatches are normally greatest within the first few hours of sunset and sunrise during the summer months.

While most mayfly, caddisfly, and stonefly hatches often occur within the first few hours of sunset and sunrise, midges can hatch all day. Try using the zebra midge nymph pattern around mid-day during the summer months (see: **FLIES** pg. 10).

Target shallow riffles, runs, and tailouts of pools during an abundant aquatic insect hatch because trout will move into these shallow areas from deep pools and runs to more easily feed.

Use small nymph patterns during low water conditions because aquatic insects that hatch during low water tend to be smaller in size.

There is normally a decrease in feeding activity directly after an abundant insect hatch because fish move directly to the bottom to rest. Fish directly on the bottom with smaller nymphs after an abundant hatch for greater success.

Fishing after heavy rain can often be excellent because rain and wind wash an abundance of food into the river. Don't be discouraged by slightly or moderately murky water; fish can still see your nymphs well enough to bite, but not clearly enough to reject them.

WINTER RIVER CHANGES

Insect activity decreases in the cooler months and aquatic insect hatches normally occur when water temperatures are highest - around the middle of the day. Since there is little surface hatch activity in the winter, nymphing is the most productive angling method.

Target deep pools and runs in the cooler months. Trout metabolic activity decreases when temperatures become too low, and they will move into deep and slow water where they do not have to fight the current.

You have to fish right on the bottom and place your nymphs almost directly in a fish's mouth in the cooler months. In order to conserve energy, trout will often move no more than one inch to take your fly in the cooler months.

COMMON NYMPHING ERRORS & SOLUTIONS

🐟 **Not using enough weight and therefore are not getting your nymphs down on the river bottom.** Your weight should tap the bottom every few seconds throughout a drift, but not drag on the bottom and move substantially slower than the current. Your nymphing rig should occasional snag the bottom (see: **WEIGHT** pg. 4, **WATER DYNAMICS** pg. 15).

🐟 **Not having your strike indicator adjusted correctly.** Depending on your nymphing rig type, your strike indicator should be one and a half to three times the water depth. If your strike indicator is too short, your nymphs will drift too high off the bottom. If your strike indicator is too long, your rig will snag on the bottom frequently, drift unnaturally, and it will be difficult to detect when a fish strikes. You must adjust your strike indicator constantly (see: **NYMPHING RIGS** pgs. 6-9)!

🐟 **Not changing your nymph patterns frequently enough.** You should switch your flies if you are not receiving any strikes because the food source that trout are feeding on can quickly change throughout a day. Even if a particular nymph worked well earlier in the day, if it hasn't recently caught a fish, switch it (see: **FLIES** pg. 10)!

🐟 **Making too much noise and fishing too close to where fish are located.** Fish will stop feeding and retreat for cover when they feel threatened. Move quietly, maintain a low profile, keep your shadow off the water, approach from downstream, and stand as far away as you can from the area you are targeting to avoid spooking fish (see: **TROUT VISION** pg. 13).

🐟 **Not detecting a fish strike.** Set the hook anytime your strike indicator behaves unnatural because strikes are often overlooked by beginners (see: **STRIKE DETECTION** pg. 27).

🐟 **Not mending your fly line.** Your nymphs will look unnatural whenever the current pulls your strike indicator and fly line sideways across the surface during a drift. You want your strike indicator to drift in a straight line downstream from where it landed and you may need to mend your fly line to accomplish this (see: **Upstream & Downstream Mend** pg. 22).

🐟 **Having too much slack line on the water's surface.** If you have too much fly line out, you will not be able to set your hook quickly enough, and with enough force to hook a fish (see: **HOOK SET** pg. 28).

🐟 **Spooking fish while casting.** Fish can see your strike indicator and fly line, so you want to land your strike indicator softly on the water and keep your fly line from drifting over fish. Fish the area closest to you first, then work your way outward (see: **TROUT VISION** pg. 13).

🐟 **Not covering enough water.** You normally need to cover a lot of ground to catch a lot of fish. Don't you dare spend all day fishing just one pool!

Special thanks to Cameron Buglione, Anthony Canino, and Brittany Duran. This book would not have been possible without your help and support.

ABOUT THE AUTHOR

Mike Canino is a resident near the Catskill Mountain region of Upstate New York and is a fisheries biologist. He received a bachelor's degree in marine biology and studied trout and salmon species in Alaska for the U.S. Fish and Wildlife Service and Alaska Department of Fish and Game. Mike is very passionate about nymphing, and has used the techniques in his guide book to catch trout across the Northeastern and Western United States, New Zealand, and Scotland. You can commonly find him in New York nymphing for trout on the West Branch Delaware River, or fishing for migratory trout and salmon in the many tributaries to Lake Ontario. Mike is very grateful to share his knowledge, and hopes his guide book has simplified the process of nymphing and will help you to catch more fish.

Follow us for the latest fly fishing news on our blog, Instagram, and Facebook!

Website & Blog: www.simplisticnymphing.com

Instagram: simplistic_nymphing

Facebook: Simplistic Nymphing
(www.facebook.com/simplisticnymphing)

CPSIA information can be obtained
at www.ICGtesting.com
Printed in the USA
LVHW070626141118
597092LV00001B/2/P

9 781722 906191